The Complete
Masterbuilt Smoker Cookbook

The Ultimate Guide for Beginners with Simple Tasty Smoking Recipes for Happy and Leisure Living

Author: Grill Leisure

Copyright © Grill Leisure

All rights reserved. No part of this guide may be reproduced in any form without permission in writing from the publisher except in the case of brief quotations embodied in critical articles or reviews.

Legal & Disclaimer

The information contained in this book and its contents is not designed to replace or take the place of any form of medical or professional advice; and is not meant to replace the need for independent medical, financial, legal or other professional advice or services, as may be required. The content and information in this book has been provided for educational and entertainment purposes only.

Table of Contents

Introduction 7

Chapter 1: Know about The Masterbuilt Smoker 8

    What is Exactly Masterbuilt Smoker? 8

    How Does it Work? 8

    A Little about The History of Masterbuilt Electric Smoker 9

    Any Difference between Grilling and Smoking? 10

    Health Care about Smoked Foods 11

Chapter 2: Top 3 Masterbuilt Smoker 13

Chapter 3: Why You Need a Masterbuilt Smoker 16

    1. Safety features 16

    2. Temperature control 16

    3. Quality Timers 16

    4. Smoking and Cooking 16

    5. Versatile cooking choices 17

    6. Ideal for inside use 17

    7. They use clean energy 17

    8. They allow you to relax 17

    9. Good for beginners 17

    10. They're easy to clean 17

Chapter 4: Most Useful Tips and Cautions 18

    1. To Brine or Not To Brine? 18

    2. Which Wood Should You Use? 18

    3. Wood Chips VS. Wood Chunks 19

    4. How to Maintain Your Smoker 20

Chapter 5: Meat Recipes 21

1. Smoked Pork Tenderloin 21

2. Delicious Smoked Pork Belly 22

3. Tasty Pork Shoulder 23

4. Smoked Pork Tenderloin with Honey Glazed 24

5. Simple Beef Roast 25

6. Sirloin Tip Roast 26

7. Herb Smoked Prime Rib 27

8. Smoked Short Ribs 28

9. Smoked Herb Marinated Lamb Skewers 29

10. Smoked Herbed Lamb Chops 30

11. Smoked Lamb Cutlets with Garlic Sauce 31

12. Smoked Molasses Lamb Chops 32

Chapter 6: Poultry Recipes 33

1. Stuffed Chicken Breast in Masterbuilt Smoker 33

2. Beer Smoked Chicken in Masterbuilt Smoker 35

3. Smoked Chicken with Apple-Ginger Marinade 36

4. Smoked turkey with flavors of mixed herbs 37

5. Smoked Game Hens in Masterbuilt Smoker 39

6. Orange Smoked Chicken 40

7. Smoked Soy Chicken Drumsticks 41

8. Delicious Honey Smoked Chicken 42

9. Smoked Buffalo Chicken Wings 43

10. Moist Wrapped Chicken Tenders 44

11. Sweet and Spicy Chicken Wings 45

12. Simple Turkey Breast 46

Chapter 7: Vegetable Recipes 47

1. Smoked Summer Vegetables 47

2. Herby Smoked Cauliflower 48

3. Smoked Green Beans with Lemon 49

4. Smoked Lemony-Garlic Artichokes 50

5. Smoked Portobello Mushrooms with Herbs de Provence 51

6. Smoky Corn on the Cob 52

7. Smoked Potato Salad 53

8. Smoked Volcano Potatoes 54

9. Groovy smoked asparagus 55

10. Smoked Squash Casserole 56

11. Smoked Eggplant 57

12. Twice Pulled Potatoes 58

Chapter 8: Snacks & Desserts 59

1. Grilled Apple Pie 59

2. Pear and Fig Upside Down Cake 60

3. Belgian Beer Brownies 61

4. Baked Lemon Meringue Pie 62

5. Smoked Peaches 64

6. Smoked Apple Crumble 65

7. Smoke Roasted Apple Crisp 66

8. Tangerine Smoked Flans 67

9. Pizza Jalapeño Poppers 69

10. Smoked Chocolate Bread Pudding 70

11. Smoked Banana Foster 71

12. Smoke Roasted Berry Crisp 72

Chapter 9: Delicious Cheese & Nuts 73

1. Smoked Cheddar Cheese 73

2. Smoked Brie Cheese 74

3. Grilled Smoked Bananas with Dark Chocolate and Toasted Hazelnuts 75
4. Garlic and Cayenne Almonds 76
5. Splendid Cheeseburger Patty 77
6. Marvelous Smoked Mac'n'Cheese 78
7. Macaroni & Cheese 79
8. Smoked Chorizo Queso 80
9. Christy's Smoked Pimento Cheese Appetizer 81
10. Smoked Rosemary Cashews 82
11. Smoked Pecans 83
12. Smoked Spiced Nuts and Seeds 84

Chapter 10: Sauces & Rubs as Bonus (Not Made By Masterbuilt Smoker) 85

1. Texas Style Brisket Rub 85
2. Montreal Steak Rub 86
3. Sage BBQ Rub 87
4. Carolina Barbeque Rub 88
5. Memphis Rub 89
6. Black Bean & Sesame Sauce 90
7. Best-Ever Chili Sauce 91
8. Quick Red Wine Sauce 92
9. Easy Mustard Sauce 93
10. Teriyaki Sauce 94

Conclusion 95

Introduction

What is good about smoked meat or fish or any other product suitable for smoking? Well, of course, the fact that all of them are tasty. And yet — they can be stored for a long time. The smoke generated during the combustion of specially selected firewood, helps preservative substances accumulate in the meat. It hardens slightly and acquires a mouth-watering appearance and a wonderful taste; a pleasant smell of smoke.

Smoking is an essential part of cooking which raises the food taste or flavor. A Smokey dish is so wonderful, when you need to cook something fascinating and something new for your friends and family.

Have you at any point longed to own a dragon? It would be a ground-breaking being, with metal skin and fire in its gut, and it would comply with the commands you give to it. Your fantasy can materialize, with the Masterbuilt Smoker that smokes a wide range of meat, with the addition of tasty woody flavors and fragrances to your meat cuts. All the flavor will be contained in your smoked meat and it will be all yours to enjoy.

The Masterbuilt Electric Smokers history traces back to 1970s initiated by Dawson McLemore. The Masterbuilt electric smokers provide good value for the money, offering you an easy way to smoke food without making a hole in your budget. If you treat your smoker carefully and following all the instructions, it will last you for a long time. If you like smoked food, then it's a good choice for you.

Furthermore, these smokers are considered to be user-friendly. You can just set the electric smoker and leave it to cook your meal for dinner. So, with the help of Masterbuilt electric smoker, be a chef of everyone's choice and show the magic of your hands.

Chapter 1: Know about The Masterbuilt Smoker

What is Exactly Masterbuilt Smoker?

An electric smoker is a beneficial kitchen equipment used to grill food without having to experience the fuss or mess brought about by a regular smoker. The Masterbuilt electric smoker is a smoker developed by the Masterbuilt Company and uses an electric heating element. Most also include a tray for wood pellets or chips, so you get the flavors from different types of smoke. There are analog and digital smokers, which give you control over the temperature. It is one of the best innovations in the culinary world as it has made smoked meals a comfort food. Now you can easily smoke your favorite meat and enjoy it quickly.

How Does it Work?

The five main parts of an electric smoker are:

- Digital control pad
- Smoker body
- Water bowl
- Drip Tray
- Wood chip bowl and lid

The heat source in an electric heater is, of course, a metallic rod. The user can control the temperature of this glowing metal rod by the thermostat. After setting the temperature anywhere between 100 to 275 degrees F and timing, the thermostat will take care of the rest as it senses and senses and maintains temperature. There is no need to worry about the meat being cooked evenly as the excellent insulation system ensures that. There is a side wood chip loader from where you can add chips, dry and soaked both can be used for a smokier, more barbecue texture and smell. The adjustable air damper helps with controlling the amount of 'smoky-ness' inside the compartment. You never have to worry about replenishing the wood chips in the chamber for temperature control as this is being directly controlled by the temperature control system. Some popular choices of wood for the chips are but alder, cherry, and plum. You will be burning almost 4 cups of chips in a 3 to 5-hour session.

Before utilizing the smoker for the first time, make sure that it is pre-seasoned. Pre-season instructions can be found in the manual of your smoker.

Usually, the smoker has a digital panel for the selection of settings like the type of meat, temperature, etc. Every new smoker has features and options that are perplexing for a new user. So it is better to familiarize yourself with the setting options before you begin. The first action to take is finding the on/off switch and press that. Next, press the 'Set Temp' button to go into temperature selection mode. Up and down arrow buttons will help with that. Press 'Set Temp' again to exit temperature mode. This feature always ensures that your meat doesn't get over or undercooked. In order to set the time, Select 'Set Time', use up and down arrows to select a number of hours and press 'Set Temp' to lock in the hour's selection and move to a number of minutes. Follow the same procedure for minutes and finally, press 'Set Time' to start cooking. One very special feature in the Masterbuilt Electric Smoker is the meat probe which is inserted in the center of the piece of meat to monitor the internal temperature which is displayed on the LED display. In case of error display, turn off the smoker, unplug the smoker and restart after waiting for 10 minutes. After every use, the smoker should be cleaned and the racks washed well with mild dish detergent. Do not use detergent in the interior of the smoker.

The smoker has ample space inside- it can accommodate 2 turkeys, 4 pork butts, 4 racks of ribs and 6 chickens at a time.

One amazing feature is that you can add flavor to the meat you're cooking by filling the removable water pan with any juicy, spicy beverage of your liking such as vinegar, lemon juice, sauce, gravy etc. The water pan is also used to keep the meat moist as it keeps getting dehydrated during the smoking process and we do not want a dry, tasteless dish at the end of the day. Using hot water will be even better for your meat. The main use of this drip tray is to collect all the fluid coming out of the meat that causes the temperature to fluctuate.

Have fun to explore many more features of your smoker to get the best flavor for your dish. The overall basic working is very simple after you have set the temperature and timing.

A Little about The History of Masterbuilt Electric Smoker

It might not be the oldest manufacturer of electric smokers, but the Masterbuilt Electric Smokers date back to the 1970s. This company is one of the long-standing brands that manufacture electric smokers. This company was built on faith, family and sheer hard work. To sum it up, in a nutshell, this company combines invention, faith and family values. What started as a simple backyard project transformed into a blooming business. It all started with Dawson McLemore. A brief history of this company is required before getting started with the information about the electric smoker. Dawson was an employee at Goodyear Tire and Rubber Company. He was working really hard to support his family. When an opportunity arose, he took it and turned his hobby of welding into a full-time job and ultimately a family business.

Any Difference between Grilling and Smoking?

The difference between grilling and smoking is huge. Grilling is a cooking method where heat is used to cook the food. The source of heat can be charcoal, wood, propane gas, or electricity. Outdoor grills mostly use charcoal, gas or wood and while cooking, you have the opportunity to infuse the flavors of the charcoal or the specific type of wood that is being used. In case of electric operated grills (i.e. the indoor grill) you will most probably be missing the infusion of woody or charcoal flavors.

A smoker is a device that makes use of smoke along with heat to cook the food. There is a wood tray that holds the wood chips that release the required smoke. The smoke is released into an airtight smoking chamber where the food to be cooked is kept. The smoke and heat released by the burning wood cooks the food at a low temperature, slowly. So, it is pretty obvious that smoked food is another version of slow cooking. The heat is not directly transferred to the food. You have to cook for a longer time (as compared to other cooking methods like oven cooking or microwave cooking) to get the food thoroughly cooked. There could also be a water tray in the smoking device which helps to create more smoke, and several types of infused liquids can be used to create flavors.

Modern-day household smokers have created an opportunity for home chef's to cook wonderful dishes, previously inaccessible, with ease. Old smokers were huge and not very convenient for domestic uses. We had to rely on restaurants for having some great smoked foods. But, gone are those days and in keeping with the demands of the customers, cooking appliance manufacturers have come up with inventions to satisfy the needs of the customers. Household smokers are easy to handle and easy to operate as well. The main materials needed for the use of a home smoker are wood chips. They are available (in various flavors) in small packages and can be bought from grocery supply stores or even online. All you need to know is how to use the chips and which ones to use for which meal you are trying to prepare. The rest of the meals can be prepared easily when you have a great recipe book (like this one!!) to follow.

Health Care about Smoked Foods

Smoked foods are not just a delicacy, but healthy. Smoked foods require minimal ingredients and spices and thus they are not only easy to cook, but also extremely good for health. However, nothing in the world is absolutely good or bad – and this applies to smoked foods as well. You need to know certain health facts about smoked foods before you dig in. As far as smoked food is concerned, they are easy to prepare and can be consumed with simple home cooked bread or just a bowl of salad. This may trigger your desire to depend completely on this kind of food on a daily basis. Stay away from this habit (we are talking of developing the habit of eating lots of smoked foods on a daily basis) and make sure that your food habit is a well-balanced one. Let us take a detailed look at the facts related to our health when we consume smoked foods.

1. **The very first thing to consider is moderation.** Smoked foods have to be consumed in moderation. Smoked foods have a high percentage of fats which are used in the cooking process. The fat that is used while preparing the smoked food is saturated in nature and we have all heard the bad news with regard to saturated fats. Lots of saturated fats in your diet can lead to serious conditions like heart disease and obesity. Some common smoked foods are sausages and salami, which we are always in love with, and can make us sick when consumed in large quantities. If you can keep your level of consumption within check, you can enjoy the great tastes of such foods without causing harm to yourself. Same theory goes for the dishes you cook (read smoke) in your smoking device. Have in moderation.
2. **Smoking is the cooking method where the ingredients (mostly meat, fishes and vegetables) are to be cured and well marinated.** Curing is the method where the meat or fish (even vegetables – though the curing process and time for vegetables is hugely different from that of the fish and meat) is preserved with salt or other curing agents like lime or vinegar. This helps to enhance the flavors as well as increase the shelf life of the same. Adding extra flavors to fish and meat is another great aspect of curing. Now, the trouble is that lots of salt has to be used while curing and this can be a health issue. This implies that cured meat or fish could be loaded with sodium. Sodium is a mineral we need in moderation to remain healthy. Unmeasured intake of sodium could lead to a sodium imbalance within the body.

Too much intake of sodium can lead to conditions like hypertension, kidney failure and heart problems.
3. **Smoked foods can become dangerous if not watched out for.** This is the case when you forget the fact of consuming in moderation and opt for the fatty rich options like the sausages over the leaner cuts of smoked meat. Obesity will be the ultimate achievement you will gain when you forget the moderation theory while consuming the smoked fatty foods.
4. **Certain smoked foods are home to deadly bacteria and other parasites.** Smoked salmon is extremely rich in nutrients and omega-3 fatty acids. This will obviously lure you to consume more. But the fact is far away from what it appears at first sight. Besides being rich in the nutrients, the smoked salmon is also the breeding ground for bacteria which can prove to be fatal. It is especially advised that pregnant women must stay away from smoked fish and meat so that they do not come in contact with the deadly parasites and cause harm to selves and their unborn babies.
5. **Smoking is a slow cooking process where the heat is not directly used to cook the food.** This implies that the heat which could have killed the harmful parasites (in case of general cooking methods) remains inactive. So, the parasites thrive and continue posing health threats. Smoking also involves cold smoking where the food (fish or meat) is first cured and then smoked in cold temperature. This method actually does not cook the food, but just uses the smoke to infuse the desired flavors in the food. This method is used primarily to enhance the flavors of the cuts of meat like the beef, pork chops, chicken breasts or fish fillets. This also implies that since the fish or meat is not cooked, the bacteria (and other parasites that may cause health hazards) are not killed or inactivated due to heat and they are obviously not destroyed simply because they were not exposed to high temperature. No matter what type of smoking method is being used to cook your food (we mean the cold one or the hot one) it is advised to be very careful in consuming smoked foods as there is always the risk of bacterial or parasitic infection.

The bottom line is that you have to be extremely careful about consuming smoked foods (whether home cooked or bought from the stores) in moderation and make sure that they are properly manufactured (if you are buying from the store) and if you have it cooked it yourself, make sure to follow the hygiene rules strictly to make your delicious food safe.

Chapter 2: Top 3 Masterbuilt Smoker

1. Masterbuilt Smoker With Front Controlling & Viewing Window, RF Remote Controlling, 40-Inch (Masterbuilt 20075315 Front Controller Smoker)

If you are looking for a top pick to add in your kitchen, then this 40-inch remote controlled Masterbuilt smoker should be your first choice. It has extra cooking space, external chip feeding chute (fuel and wood, both) and a nicely-sized internal drip tray. This smoker is a total delight for customers who love cooking with great functionality. Other features of this smoker are; 4-rack system, curvaceous back-ends, and easy-to-use functionality. So, you can say that this smoker is highly convenient and value for your hard-earned money. It will definitely rely on your expectations.

2. The 30-Inch Masterbuilt Black-colored Electric &Analog Smoker (Masterbuilt 20070210 Electric Smoker)

If you desire style in an electric smoker, then, Masterbuilt offers a 30-inch analog electric smoker is your sure bet. This beautiful smokehouse unit accompanies the look of a smokehouse that incorporates three difference racks for the generation of smoke without compromising with the lack of space.

There is also the luxury of a controllable thermostat that lets you control the temperature at your will without much difficulty. Moreover, the unit offers a pre-installed thermometer that will ensure that your smoking setting is not exceeded. This design also encompasses a tray made of wood chips inside the unit with a supporting water pan. Masterbuilt electric analog smoking unit is also a representation of the company's intro model. In appearance, it looks like a bare bone, but it is a perfect design that executes the job of a smoking unit.

However, it is prudent to note that an individual will need to unlock the cabinet to add in more smoke chips when needed. This, unfortunately, may lead to the loss of some heat in the smoking process. This is the only perceived shortcoming of this model; aside from that, it is a great buy.

This is a smoking and cooking unit for real with a minimum supporting temperature of 100 degrees F and a maximum 400 degrees F. Do note that you can keep the complete smoking process quite clear and easy if you use aluminum pans that are disposable after smoking the meat. The problem of having to scrub and scrape your cooking utensils is thereby eliminated.

3. Masterbuilt 30-Inch Digital & Electric Smoke (Black Colored) With Top Controller (Masterbuilt 20070910 Electric Digital Smoker)

This model is an upgraded version of the analog model discussed above, that incorporates a few add-ons for an impressive smoking experience. Here too, the smokehouse device accompanies the style used for designing cabinets with the benefits of digital regulators for better precision while reading the temperature and, thankfully, a wood chip feeding system present outside the unit.
Most issues arising from the usage of some smokers have to do with temperature control. When this problem surfaces, the food is either overcook to your displeasure or completely burnt to your chagrin. The digital controls included in this model will make sure that a precise temperature (that the desired temperature) is maintained 24/7.
The panel for input settings digitally boasts a commendable timer system featuring a 24-hour clock that offers an autonomous switch off the system when your food is cooked. Issues of overcooking are out of the equation. It also has the benefit of wood chips feeding from the outside into the electric smoker. You, therefore, will not undergo the ritual of opening up the main cabinet when you want to refuel. The advantage here is that you will not lose heat when there is a need to refuel the unit. Masterbuilt offers this profound digital and electric smoker accompanied by a top regulator that works well within the temperature scale of 100 to 275 degrees F. You must note at this temperature range that the unit is not meant for fast and hot smoking. Nevertheless, this model is ideal for lower temperatures and is suitable for BBQ, making jerky and cooking some delicious fish.

Chapter 3: Why You Need a Masterbuilt Smoker

Like with any other smoker, the preparatory work makes all the difference when it comes to the end result. Maintaining and cleaning it is quite easy. You will learn more later and also the different tricks that will help you smoke food like a maestro. Regardless of the manufacturer, the electric smokers will help you in cooking food that has a mild smoky flavor. The flavor that you might get from if you cook on a concrete block or even a brick pit would be quite different. That being said, this appliance does help you get perfectly smoked food. You can also amp up the smoke level from this by selecting different woods for smoking. Woods that have a fruity flavor like apple, peach, or cherry will provide a mild smoky flavor.

There are quite a few reasons why people are choosing electric smokers over traditional methods. Here are a few benefits of owning an electric smoker:

1. Safety features

Just like the common dangers that are associated with using burning wood or charcoal, there is always the chance that stray embers cause an outburst of fire. The electric smoker is safe since there are no embers.

2. Temperature control

Unlike traditional charcoal or gas smokers that give little or no control over the temperature, an electric smoker allows you to regulate the heat settings, so that whatever temperature you have set is maintained throughout the cooking process.

3. Quality Timers

Electric smokers have control timers of high caliber. After setting the timer, it automatically closes, which implies you can "set and forget." You won't need to be opening the door to monitor the progress.

4. Smoking and Cooking

With regards to speed, electric smokers are the quickest alternatives for smoking, and equitably spread the heat. The final outcome is your food being perfectly cooked with a tasty smoky flavor.

5. Versatile cooking choices

You can prepare a variety of food items from beef, turkey, chicken, and pork to cheese, sausages, nuts and bacon.

6. Ideal for inside use

Unlike gas and charcoal, many electric smokers can be used inside in the kitchen or on a balcony since they do not generate a lot of smoke. But never fear— they will generate just the right amount of smoke to flavor your food.

7. They use clean energy

When you use gas or charcoal as your heat source, the fumes generated are "dirty." They are the kind of fumes that contribute to climate change. There are also a lot of housing complexes like townhouses and apartments that won't let you use gas or charcoal. Electric smokers use clean energy, and release significantly fewer contaminants into the air and into your food.

8. They allow you to relax

With traditional smokers, you are in charge of regulating the temperature by feeding it fuel. With electric smokers, the heating source is always consistent. All you have to do is set the temp you want and wait. That gives you time to focus on other parts of your meal or spend time with your friends and family while the food cooks. You can even set an electric smoker to cook food overnight or while you're away from the house.

9. Good for beginners

If you don't have experience barbecuing, an electric smoker is one of the best ways to get started. You don't have to know a lot about how much wood to use or how to regulate the smoker temperature to produce great food. Electric smokers are also much safer, so you don't have to be scared of it.

10. They're easy to clean

Because there's no messy charcoal or gas involved, cleaning an electric smoker is easy. There isn't much fuel residue to deal with, and because most electric smokers are made of stainless steel, wiping off surfaces is fast.

Chapter 4: Most Useful Tips and Cautions

1. To Brine or Not To Brine?

Smoked meat needs a good brine. Brines are used to make the meat more water-absorbent. The salt protects the meat proteins against moisture loss, so the meat stays juicy throughout the smoking process. You get the best results by brining for 10-12 hours.

The most basic brine is just water and salt, but most recipes will include other spices and sugar to balance out the saltiness. After a brine and before smoking, you usually rinse off the meat.

2. Which Wood Should You Use?

Once you have an electric smoker, what wood to use is the next consideration. There are two types of wood: softwoods and hardwoods. Softwoods include hemlock, redwood, pine, spruce, and fir. They burn fast and are not typically used for smoking. Hardwoods, however, are the fruit and nut woods that help make meat delicious.

So, yes, if you want a single-word answer, then the most flexible type of wood is hickory, since it goes well with poultry, fish, ham, beef, and pork, giving them an extra layer of bacon taste, but not lamb, which demands mesquite. Poultry can go well with every wood type due to the inherent mild taste of white meat. None of this is set in stone, though, so feel free to test everything out and boldly smoke a combo no one has smoked before.

Choosing the right hardwood for what you're cooking is essential. Here's a list of descriptions:

Apple
Light and sweet, this wood is popular for pulled pork, ham, and chicken. It's considered a "medium-flavored" wood, and isn't quite strong enough for beef.

Alder
Another sweet wood, alder is popular with salmon and other fish. It also makes tasty chicken. It has a slightly smoky flavor mixed in with the sweetness.

Cherry
Good for a variety of meats including pork and poultry, cherry wood is sweet and fruity. It's often mixed with smokier woods (like hickory) to add depth. It adds a mahogany color to meat, as well.

Citrus
Orange, lemon, and grapefruit wood are all mild and very fruity. They mellow out stronger woods and work with any type of meat.

Hickory
The gold standard for smoking woods, hickory as a bold flavor that's best with lamb, beef, and pork. It adds a bacon-like flavor to meats. If it's too strong for you, mix with apple or citrus wood.

Maple
Sweet like the syrup, maple wood is relatively mild and is popular for smoking chicken, vegetables, and even cheese. The smoke darkens meat.

Mesquite
A very strong-flavored wood, mesquite reigns in Texas BBQ. It burns hot and fast, and goes best with beef and pork. It's usually mixed with a milder wood.

Oak
Oak also burns hot, but has a milder flavor than mesquite. It blends with other woods well and works best with beef and lamb.

Pecan
Technically a type of hickory wood, pecan is a bit milder. It burns cool, so it's really good for long cooking times. It can become bitter if used too long, however, so be careful.

Walnut
Strong and bitter, walnut works with bold meats like beef or wild game. It's mostly used as a blender with other milder woods.

3. Wood Chips VS. Wood Chunks

Wood Chips
Chips are tiny wood pieces meant for small and blasts of smoke. Even when soaked in water, the chips burn very fast, smoke and vanish within a short period. They are good when the smoking doesn't take long and you need to add little amounts of smoke flavor. There are some smokers designed for chips and you can't use chunks in the units.

Wood Chunks
Chunks are expansive hardwood pieces less than 2 inches. They create smoke for an extended timespan. Good when smoking for a while to get more smoke without running out. Remember to check if your smoker supports the use of wood chunks.

4. How to Maintain Your Smoker

Read the instructions.
Each smoker has its own specific functions and different operating directions. The company develops a lot of models, each with its own peculiarities, pros and cons. So you need to read the manual attentively to understand all about your smoker.

Preseason a new electric smoker.
Before using your smoker for the first time, you need to season it. First of all, coat the racks and inside surfaces with cooking oil. Then set your smoker to 275°F and leave it for about 2 hours. After that you can turn the smoker off and open the hood to let it cool.

Prepare your meat.
Season meat with salt, pepper, and other spices, or leave it for a while in a marinade.

Preheat your smoker
It's a mistake beginners often make: to put the meat into the smoker immediately after it is turned on. The electric smoker should reach a certain temperature first, and only then can you put the meat or other food into it. Do not forget to add water and wood chips. For your safety, wear special gloves. You will need about 4 cups (946.35 ml) of wood chips for every 3 to 5 hours of smoking time when using the Masterbuilt electric smoker.

Monitor the internal temperature of smoking.
It is easy to control the temperature of the electric smokers. Some of them have a dial so you can turn the temperature up or down, and others are set at an exact temperature point, for example, 250°F. While smoking, the temperature is the most important element for your success. Most electric smokers have an internal temperature gauge. If there is no such device, you can use temperature probes or wireless smoker temperature monitors to keep an eye on the cooking process.

If you see rust on the outside of the unit, scrub the spots with steel wool and paint them over, but maintenance of the interior demands special care. Take a napkin and dab it in cooking oil. Slide the napkin all over the interior of the Masterbuilt Smoker, including the grates and inside smoker door. Set the water pan in place, but do not put any water in it. Fill the flame disk bowl with plenty of charcoal (7-8 lbs.), light the smoker and close the door.

Chapter 5: Meat Recipes

1. Smoked Pork Tenderloin

Prep time: 10 minutes
Servings: 2
Ingredients:
1 pork tenderloin
¼ c. BBQ sauce
3 tbsps. dry rub
Preparations:
Heat the smoker to 225 F/107 C.
Rub spice mix over the pork tenderloin.
Place meat in the smoker and smoke until internal temperature reaches 145 F/62 C about 3 hours.
Brush BBQ sauce over the pork when is about half hour is left to go in the smoker.
Serve and enjoy.
Nutritional Information:
Calories: 405
Fat: 8.1 g
Carbs: 15.8 g
Protein: 59.4 g

2. Delicious Smoked Pork Belly

Prep time: 15 minutes
Servings: 10
Ingredients:
5 lbs. pork belly
1 c. dry rub
3 tbsps. olive oil
For sauce:
2 tbsps. honey
3 tbsps. butter
1 c. BBQ sauce
Preparations:
Preheat the smoker to 250 F/121 C.
Add pork cubes, dry rub, and olive oil into the bowl and mix well.
Place pork cubes into the smoker and smoke uncover for 3 hours.
Remove pork cubes from smoker and place on foil pan.
Add honey, butter and BBQ sauce and stir well.
Cover pan with foil and place back into the smoker.
Cook pork for another 90 minutes.
After 90 minutes remove the foil.
Close the lid to the smoker and smoke for 15 minutes or until sauce thickens.
Serve and enjoy.
Nutritional Information:
Calories 1164
Fat 68.8 g
Carbs 12.5 g
Protein 104.7 g

3. Tasty Pork Shoulder

Prep time: 10 minutes
Servings: 12
Ingredients:
8 lbs. pork shoulder
For rub:
1 tsp. dry mustard
1 tsp. black pepper
1 tsp. cumin
1 tsp. cayenne pepper
1 tsp. oregano
1/3 c. kosher salt
¼ c. garlic powder
½ c. paprika
1/3 c. brown sugar
2/3 c. sugar
Preparations:
Brine pork for 18 hours.
Pull pork from brine and set aside for 1 hour.
Rub mustard all over the meat.
Combine together all rub ingredients and rub over the meat.
Wrap meat and leave for overnight.
Smoke meat at 250 F/121 C for 6 hours.
Pull pork from grill and wrap in foil.
Return pork to grill and cook for another 6 hours at 195 F/90 C.
Shred and serve.
Nutritional Information:
Calories: 965
Fat: 65.4 g
Carbs: 19.9 g
Protein: 71.6 g

4. Smoked Pork Tenderloin with Honey Glazed

Prep time: 10 minutes
Servings: 6
Ingredients:
3 lbs. pork tenderloin
1 tsp. ground cinnamon
½ c. brown sugar
¼ c. honey
Preparations:
Add cinnamon, brown sugar and honey in microwave safe bowl and mix well.
Place bowl in microwave and microwave for 15 seconds.
Spread cinnamon mixture all over pork tenderloin.
Place pork in the smoker and smoke at 250 F/121 C.
After one-hour flip pork and smoke continue for 4 hours to 165 F/73 C.
Serve and enjoy.
Nutritional Information:
Calories: 414
Fat: 8 g
Carbs: 23.8 g
Protein: 59.4 g

5. Simple Beef Roast

Prep time: 15 minutes
Servings: 6
Ingredients:
2 lbs. beef roast
1 tbsp. ground black pepper
1 tbsp. salt
1 tbsp. olive oil
Preparations:
Heat your smoker to 225 F/107 C.
Coat beef roast with olive oil and season with pepper and salt.
Place in smoker for 60 minutes or until internal temperature reaches 130 F/54 C.
Wrap meat in foil and set aside for 30 minutes.
Cut into strips and serve.
Nutritional Information:
Calories: 304
Fat: 11.8 g
Carbs: 0.7 g
Protein: 46 g

6. Sirloin Tip Roast

Prep time: 20 minutes
Servings: 6
Ingredients:
2 lbs. sirloin tip roast
For marinade:
½ tsp. black pepper
1 tsp. chili powder
1 tbsp. minced onion
1 tsp. minced garlic
½ c. brown sugar
½ c. soy sauce
½ c. Worcestershire sauce
1 tsp. salt
Preparations:
Add roast into the ziplock bag.
Combine together all marinade ingredients and pour into the ziplock bag.
Seal bag and place in refrigerator for 3 hours.
Preheat the smoker at 250 F/121 C.
Place marinated roast into the smoker and cook for 4 hours or until internal temperature reaches 155 F/68 C.
Serve and enjoy.
Nutritional Information:
Calories: 422
Fat: 18.1 g
Carbs: 18.2 g
Protein: 42.9 g

7. Herb Smoked Prime Rib

Prep time: 10 minutes
Servings: 8
Ingredients:
5 lbs. prime rib
2 tbsps. Black pepper
¼ c. olive oil
2 tbsps. Salt
For herb paste:
¼ c. olive oil
1 tbsp. fresh sage
1 tbsp. fresh thyme
1 tbsp. fresh rosemary
3 garlic cloves
Preparations:
Add all herb ingredients into the blender and blend until combined.
Preheat the smoker to 225 F/ 107 C.
Coat rib with olive oil and season with pepper and salt.
Place season rib roast into the smoker and cook for 4 hours.
Remove rib from smoker and set aside for 30 minutes.
Cut into the slices and serve.
Nutritional Information:
Calories: 936
Fat: 81.4 g
Carbs: 2 g
Protein: 46.9 g

8. Smoked Short Ribs

Prep time: 20 minutes
Servings: 6
Ingredients:
3 lbs. short ribs
½ c. dry rub
¼ c. olive oil
½ c. ground black pepper
½ c. kosher salt
For spritz:
1/3 c. Worcestershire sauce
1/3 c. dry red wine
1/3 c. beef broth
For braising:
2 tbsps. butter
1 tbsp. rub
1 c. beef broth
1 c. dry red wine
Preparations:
Heat your smoker to 225 F/107 C with wood chips.
Season meat with black pepper and salt.
Place seasoned ribs into the smoker for 2 hours.
After 2 hours spritz ribs after every 30 minutes for 2 hours.
Combine together all braising ingredients into the aluminum pan.
Add ribs to the aluminum pan and cover the pan with foil.
Place pan in the smoker and cook for about 2 hours.
Once internal temperature reaches 205 F/96 C then removes meat from smoker and set aside for 15 minutes.
Remove ribs from pan and serve.
Nutritional Information:
Calories: 1060
Fat: 94.7 g
Carbs: 6.4 g
Protein: 33.3 g

9. Smoked Herb Marinated Lamb Skewers

Prep time: 15 minutes
Servings: 6
Ingredients:
Marinade
1/3 c. olive oil
2 crushed garlic cloves
1 lemon
½ tsp. cumin
1 tsp. fresh thyme
1 tsp. dried oregano
1 tsp. rosemary sprig
Salt
Pepper
Meat
3 lbs. lamb legs
Preparations:
To make the marinade whisk all the ingredients a large bowl, .
Cut meat into chunks and set aside.
Add meat and toss to coat.
Take a plastic wrap and cover the bowl. Refrigerate overnight.
Remove the meat from the bowl and pat dry on paper towel.
Skewer the meat onto a metal branch.
Place skewers in foil and wrap well.
Preheat smoker to 225°F and add wood chips (hickory).
Place the meat on the top stand and give smoke until internal temperature reaches 150°F.
Serve hot.
Nutrition information:
Calories: 567.72
Total Fat: 42.7g
Total Carbs: 1.43g
Protein: 42.32g

10. Smoked Herbed Lamb Chops

Prep time: 20 minutes
Servings: 8
Ingredients:
12 lamb chops
3 garlic cloves
3 tsp. basil leaves
3 tsp. marjoram leaves
3 tsp. thyme leaves
Pepper
Preparations:
Sprinkle lamb chops lightly with pepper.
In a bowl mix herbs and mashed garlic and rub into chops. Cover well, and chill at least two hours.
Remove out of the refrigerator just 45 minutes before you want to smoke it.
Preheat smoker to 225°F and add wood chips (hickory).
Place meat on the top rack and give smoke until internal temperature reaches 150°F.
Remove the chops and let cool 15 minutes before serving.
Nutrition information:
Calories: 469.84
Total Fat: 32.22g
Total Carbs: 1.09g
Protein: 41.24g

11. Smoked Lamb Cutlets with Garlic Sauce

Prep time: 10 minutes
Servings: 10
Ingredients:
6 cloves garlic
2 tbsps. Apple cider vinegar
½ c. water
¼ c. extra-virgin olive oil
1 tsp. salt
1 tsp. black pepper
4 lbs. lamb cutlets
Preparations:
In a bowl, combine together minced garlic, vinegar, water, olive oil, and salt and pepper to taste.
Rub lamb cutlets generously and refrigerate for 4 hours.
Remove out of the refrigerator just 45 minutes before you want to smoke it.
Preheat smoker to 225°F and add wood chips (hickory).
Place the meat on the top rack and give smoke until internal temperature reaches 150°F.
Remove the chops and let cool 15 minutes before serving.
Serve.
Nutritional Information:
Calories: 419.3
Total Fat: 28.77g
Total Carbs: 0.82g
Protein: 36.77g 74

12. Smoked Molasses Lamb Chops

Prep time: 10 minutes
Servings: 4
Ingredients:
½ c. dry white wine
1 c. molasses or honey
4 tbsp. minced fresh mint
Salt
Pepper
2 lbs. lamb
Preparations:
Combine molasses, wine, fresh mint, salt, and pepper to taste in a bowl.
Season cut side of boned lamb with salt and pepper, then spread with molasses mixture; roll and tie lamb.
Brush outer surface with molasses mixture.
Preheat smoker to 225°F.
Lay your meat on the top of rack then give smoke until internal temperature reaches 150°F.
Remove the chops and let cool 15 minutes before serving.
Nutritional information:
Calories: 516.86
Total Fat: 11.54g
Total Carbs: 70.84g
Protein: 46.94g

Chapter 6: Poultry Recipes

1. Stuffed Chicken Breast in Masterbuilt Smoker

Prep time: 12 minutes
Servings: 4
Ingredients:
1 c. Chopped crawfish
1/3 c. chopped red Bell pepper
¼ c. chopped Green onion
1/3 c. chopped Parsley
1 c. shredded Cheese blend
½ c. Mayonnaise
2 tsps. Cajun Hot Sauce
2 tsps. Cajun seasoning
4 boneless Chicken breasts
½ c. Moppin' Sauce
Preparations:
To prepare the Crawfish-stuffed chicken, please ensure that you bring fresh chicken breast just before cooking. It will keep the prepared dish fresh for long.
Now, let us prepare the brine. To prepare it, take a large and deep pot. Into the pot, add ½ gallon water, kosher salt (1/2 cup), and brown sugar (1/3 cup). Add the chicken breast and leave the whole in the refrigerator for a night.
Take out the chicken breasts soaked overnight in brine. Take a paper towel and pat it dry.
Leave the chicken aside and prepare the stuffing. To prepare the stuffing, take the boiled Crawfish, Green Onion, Red Pepper, Cheese and Parsley in a bowl. Add in the hot sauce and Mayonnaise. Give it a good hand-mix and keep it aside.
To prepare the stuffed chicken, you would need to soften the breasts. To do this, wrap the breasts in a plastic film and use a mallet.
Beat the chicken breasts slowly, so that all the vacuum is removed from the chicken breasts. Remember, you must gently soften it, not tear it.
Now, remove the film from the soften chicken breasts and sprinkle Cajun Seasoning over it. With your hands, nicely rub the seasoning over chicken breasts so that it is nicely seasoned.

Now, take the stuffing (approximately 4-5 tbsps), or depending upon the size of the chicken breast and keep it on the top.

Roll up the chicken breasts and nicely seal it so that the mixture does not pour out.

Meanwhile, prepare the Masterbuilt smoker and add Sassafras woodchips. The temperature of the smoker should be 275 degrees Fahrenheit.

Into the heated smoker, place the rolled-up Cajun seasoned chicken breasts.

Insert a thermometer probe to check the internal temperature. When the temperature reaches, 160 degrees Fahrenheit, wipe it off with the Moppin' Sauce. The chicken will take about an hour and a half to reach the desired temperature of 160 degrees.

Now, cook it for 30 minutes more until the temperature reaches, 165 degrees F.

After 30 minutes, remove Chicken Breasts from Masterbuilt Smoker and keep it aside for about 10-15 minutes.

Serve it and enjoy!

Nutritional Information:
Calories: 184.8
Carbs: 20.5 g
Protein: 19.9 g
Fat: 2.0 g

2. Beer Smoked Chicken in Masterbuilt Smoker

Prep time: 13 minutes Servings: 6

Ingredients:
1 Whole chicken
¼ c. Dry Rub
1 can Beer
3 c. Marinade

Preparations:
Start by rinsing the chicken cavity and removing giblets.
Take the dry rub or seasoning of your choice and properly rub inside and out of the chicken.
While rubbing, press the seasoning onto the surface of the chicken and allow it to rest in the refrigerator for an hour.
Meanwhile, prepare the Masterbuilt Smoker and empty the beer can in the drip pan.
In the can, fill up the marinade and put that can into the cavity of the chicken.
Now, keep aside the chicken and prepare the Masterbuilt Electric Smoker. You have to keep it on indirect heat mode and use the woodchips of your liking.
For this particular recipe, I would recommend, Applewood; however, if that is unavailable, you can choose one from, Hickory, Mesquite, or Oakwood.
Going further, maintain the temperature of the smoker something between 225 degrees F and 275 degrees F.
It is time now to place the chicken on Smoker Grill with Beer Can as the base. Cook the chicken for at least 3 hours.
If you have used a dripping pan filled with beer and water, that is great; but if you have not done so, then try basting the chicken with the marinade you have.
Also, to see the internal temperature of the chicken, poke a thermometer in the thickest part of the meat and wait for the thermometer to read 165 degrees F.
If the thermometer reads 165 degrees F, your chicken in beer is ready.
Now, once done, remove the chicken from the smoker and let it rest for additional 20 minutes.
After 20 minutes, take out your knife and fork and just binge on.

Nutritional Information:
Calories: 127.6
Carbs: 0.3g
Protein: 21.6g
Fat: 0.8g

3. Smoked Chicken with Apple-Ginger Marinade

Prep time: 10 minutes   Servings: 6

Ingredients:

½ c. Rice Vinegar
½ c. Apple juice
3 tbsps. Tamari sauce
3 tbsps. ketchup

1 piece Fresh ginger
2 tbsps. Dijon mustard
2 tbsps. Olive oil
¼ tsp. Black pepper

1 Lemon
3 lbs. Chicken
1 can Beer

Preparations:

Take a small mixing bowl and mix all ingredients, including rice vinegar, apple juice, tamari sauce, natural ketchup, ginger, Dijon Mustard, Olive oil, black pepper, and lemon.

The prepared mixture is marinade which you will use to marinade the chicken.

So, take the chicken and empty its cavity. Rinse it with running water and nicely dry it using the paper towel. Once dried, use the marinade to cover the chicken. Put that marinated chicken in the refrigerator and forget for 2 hours. For better flavor, you can even leave it for 24 hours.

Now, on the next day, take out the chicken from the refrigerator and keep the rest of the marinade aside. You can later use it while smoking the chicken for basting.

So, as your chicken is marinated, you will now require the smoker to smoke it finally. Therefore, start by heating the smoker and placing the woodchips for flavor. I would recommend Applewood.

The temperature of the Masterbuilt Smoker should be 250 degrees F and the mode should be direct. Now, place the chicken on the rack and use a drip pan filled with beer and water.

While the chicken is being smoked, keep an eye on the doneness of the chicken. You will require 185 degrees F as an internal temperature for the doneness of the chicken. To check, you will need to insert a thermometer probe in the thickest part of the chicken.

Once the internal temperature is 185 degrees F, the chicken is ready.

You can enjoy it with your family and friends.

Nutritional Information:

Calories: 127.6
Carbs: 0.3g

Protein: 21.6g
Fat: 0.8g

4. Smoked turkey with flavors of mixed herbs

Prep time: 20 minutes
Serving size: 6
Ingredients:
14 lbs. Turkey
2 tsps. Dried thyme
1 tsp. Powdered sage
2 tbsps. Dried oregano
2 tbsps. Paprika
2 tbsps. Sea salt
1½ tbsps. Black pepper
1 tsp. Dried rosemary
1 tsp. Onion
1 tsp. Garlic powder
½ orange
¼ c. Olive oil
½ c. Apple Cider
½ c. Water
Preparations:
To prepare the smoked turkey, you will require a perfect size of Turkey that could fit in your electric smoker. Once you buy the turkey, you will require to thaw it nice and slow.
Although, if you choose a refrigerated turkey, you will still have to leave it for 3 days to completely thaw.
Once the process is complete, clean the turkey and remove giblets and neck. After cleaning it, rinse it with water and let it dry.
Meanwhile, it is kept to dry, prepare the brine mixing ½ cup or sugar and salt to water. It should be measured every gallon until the turkey is fully submerged. Allow the turkey to rest for 14 hours.
After 14 hours, take the turkey out of the brine and rinse it. The rinsing should be done with cold water. As you have rinsed the turkey, dry it with the help of a paper towel and keep it aside.
Meanwhile, prepare the Masterbuilt Smoker for direct heating at a temperature of 225 degrees F.

As the smoker is heating, prepare the herb mixture by mixing all the herbs in a mixing bowl. With this prepared mix, rub the turkey all over the outside surface. For better flavor, force the dry rub on the skin of Turkey.

Also, for the second layering of rub, add the EVOO and zest of an orange in the herb mix. Again, nicely apply the seasoning all over the outside surface and let the turkey rest.

Meanwhile, you take a water pan and add cider vinegar with an equal quantity of water. Place the water pan in the bottom of Masterbuilt Smoker. The pan must be half filled.

Also, place a drip just a shelf below Turkey so that it could collect all the juices and drippings during the smoking process. Last but not the least, add the Applewood chips in the box and the smoker is ready to place the turkey.

Now, while it is the time to place the turkey in the smoker, you will have to tightly tuck the wings beneath the turkey. After tucking the wings, place it on the rack and seal the door.

The timer of the smoker should be set at 6.5 hours. To check the doneness of the turkey, insert a thermometer probe in the thickest part and wait for it to display 165 degrees F.

While the smoking process is on, check the turkey every hour for a smoke; if you see less smoke, add more Applewood chips.

After 6.5 hours, when the meat thermometer reads 165 degrees F, remove the smoked turkey and let it rest on cutting board for 20 minutes.

After 20 minutes, carve beautifully and juices pieces of turkey and serve.

You can serve herb-smoked sweet potatoes as a side dish to this flavorful turkey.

Nutritional Information:
Calories: 276.4
Carbs: 0.1g
Protein: 30.7g
Fat: 16.2g

5. Smoked Game Hens in Masterbuilt Smoker

Prep time: 15 minutes
Servings: 8

Ingredients:
4 Game Hens
¼ c. Olive oil
1 Orange
4 tsps. Sea salt
2 tsps. Black pepper
2 tsps. Dried thyme
Fruitwood chips
Water
Butcher's twine

Preparations:
Clean the hens and rinse them with water. After rinsing them with water, use a paper towel to dry them.
After that, allow the hens to stay at room temperature; you can leave them for maximum 30-minutes.
While the chicken is resting, prepare the seasoning. Set the Masterbuilt smoker to 250 degrees F. For the smoky flavors, add Fruitwood chips to chip tray and add water to the water bowl. It should be filled up to halfway.
Now, as you have already prepared the seasoning, combine it with EVOO and rub in the cavity and on the outside surface of each hen.
After rubbing the seasoning, stuff each hen with oranges, 3 quarters and tie the legs with twine.
Place the hens on the smoker rack and nicely tuck their wings under their trunk.
Smoke them for 2 and a half hours and check for internal temperature. It should be 165 degrees F.
If required keep adding the woodchips for continuous smoking.
Once done, remove hens and let them rest for 20 minutes.
Discard the organs and cut them into halves.
Serve them with side dishes of your choice.

Nutritional Information:
Calories: 160
Carbs: 0g
Protein: 14g
Fat: 11g

6. Orange Smoked Chicken

Prep time: 10 minutes
Servings: 3
Ingredients:
12 oz. chicken breasts
For rub:
2 tbsps. Chicken rub seasoning
For marinade:
1 tbsp. garlic powder
½ c. soy sauce
2 c. orange juice
Preparations:
Add chicken and marinade ingredients into the ziplock bag and mix well.
Place chicken bag in the refrigerator for overnight.
Preheat the smoker to 250 F/121 C using apple wood chips.
Remove chicken from marinade and rub chicken seasoning over the chicken.
Place chicken in smoker and smoker for 2 hours or until internal temperature reaches 165 F/73 C.
Serve and enjoy.
Nutritional Information:
Calories: 322
Fat: 8.8g
Carbs: 22.5g
Protein: 37.1g

7. Smoked Soy Chicken Drumsticks.

Prep time: 10 minutes
Servings: 4
Ingredients:
3½ lbs. chicken thighs
2 c. apple juice
¼ c. BBQ spice
½ c. soy sauce
½ c. Italian salad dressing
Preparations:
Add chicken, BBQ spice, soy sauce, and Italian salad dressing in a ziplock bag and mix well.
Place chicken bag in the refrigerator for overnight.
Preheat the smoker to 250 F/121 C using apple wood.
Remove chicken from marinade and place in smoker and smoke for 4 hours.
After every 30 minutes misting with apple juice.
Serve and enjoy.
Nutritional Information:
Calories: 928
Fat: 37.9g
Carbs: 23g
Protein: 117g

8. Delicious Honey Smoked Chicken

Prep time: 15 minutes
Servings: 4
Ingredients:
16 oz. chicken breasts, skinless and boneless
For seasoning:
1 tsp. onion powder
1 tsp. garlic powder
1 tsp. Chinese five spice
For marinade:
2 tbsps. soy sauce
¼ c. honey
¾ c. orange juice
Preparations:
Add all marinade ingredients to the microwave safe bowl and microwave for 30 seconds.
Add chicken and marinade into the ziplock bag and mix well.
Place marinated chicken in refrigerator for 1 hour.
Combine together all seasoning ingredients and set aside.
Preheat the smoker to 250 F/121 C using apple wood.
Remove chicken from marinade and sprinkle with seasoning mixture from both the sides.
Place chicken in smoker and smoke for 30 minutes then flip chicken and smoke for another 20 minutes or until internal temperature reaches 155 F/68 C.
Serve and enjoy.
Nutritional Information:
Calories: 310
Fat: 8.5g
Carbs: 23.9g
Protein: 33.9g

9. Smoked Buffalo Chicken Wings

Prep time: 20 minutes
Servings: 8
Ingredients:
5 lbs. chicken wings
Pepper
Salt
2 tbsps. Butter
1 c. red hot sauce
Preparations:
Place chicken wings into the refrigerator for 3 hours.
Preheat the smoker to 225 F/107 C.
Remove chicken wings from refrigerator and coat with little olive oil.
Season chicken wings with pepper and salt.
Place chicken wings in the smoker for 1 hour.
After 1-hour increase temperature to 350 F/176 C and smoke for another 30 minutes.
In a bowl, combine together sauce ingredients.
Add smoked chicken wings into the bowl and toss well.
Serve and enjoy.
Nutritional Information:
Calories: 567
Fat: 24g
Carbs: 0.5g
Protein: 82.2g

10. Moist Wrapped Chicken Tenders

Prep time: 10 minutes
Servings: 5
Ingredients:
1 lb. chicken tenders
1 tbsp. chili powder
1/3 c. brown sugar
1 tsp. garlic powder
1 tsp. onion powder
1 tsp. paprika
½ tsp. Italian seasoning
10 bacon slices
½ tsp. pepper
½ tsp. salt
Preparations:
Preheat the smoker to 350 F/176 C.
In a bowl, combine together Italian seasoning, garlic powder, onion powder, paprika, pepper, and salt.
Add chicken tenders to the bowl and toss well.
Wrap each chicken tenders with a bacon slice.
Mix together chili powder and brown sugar and sprinkle over the wrapped chicken.
Place wrapped the chicken in smoker and smoke for 30 minutes.
Serve and enjoy.
Nutritional Information:
Calories: 247
Fat: 7.9g
Carbs: 11.5g
Protein: 26.7g

11. Sweet and Spicy Chicken Wings

Prep time: 20 minutes
Servings: 8

Ingredients:
5 lbs. chicken wings
3 tbsps. apple juice
½ c. BBQ sauce
1 c. honey
1 tbsp. garlic powder
1 tbsp. chili powder
1 tbsp. onion powder
2½ tbsps. black pepper
1 tbsp. salt

Preparations:
Combine together black pepper, seasoned salt, garlic powder, chili powder, and onion powder.
Add chicken wings into the ziplock bag then pour dry rub mixture over the chicken and mix well.
Place chicken bag into the refrigerator for overnight.
Preheat the smoker to 225 F/107 C using apple wood chips.
Place chicken wings in smoker and smoke for 20 minutes.
After 20 minutes turn chicken and smoke for another 25 minutes or until internal temperature reach 165 F/73 C.
Meanwhile, in a small saucepan combine together BBQ sauce, honey, and apple juice and cook over medium heat.
Remove chicken wings from smoker and toss with BBQ sauce mixture.
Return chicken wings into the smoker and smoke for another 25 minutes.
Serve hot and enjoy.

Nutritional Information:
Calories: 748
Fat: 21.4g
Carbs: 54.4g
Protein: 82.8g

12. Simple Turkey Breast

Prep time: 15 minutes
Servings: 8
Ingredients:
5 lbs. turkey breast
½ c. chicken rub seasoning
Preparations:
Preheat your smoker to 225 F/107 C using wood chips.
Wash turkey and pat dry using a paper towel.
Rub chicken seasoning over the turkey and place in smoker.
Smoke turkey about 5 hours or until internal temperature reaches 165 F/73 C.
Serve and enjoy.
Nutritional Information:
Calories: 310
Fat: 5g
Carbs: 14.9g
Protein: 48.9g

Chapter 7: Vegetable Recipes

1. Smoked Summer Vegetables

Prep Time: 30 minutes
Servings: 4
Ingredients:
Summer squash
2 zucchini
1 onion
2 cups mushrooms
2 cups French-cut green beans
Preparations:
Wash thoroughly and slice squash, onion, and zucchini, mushrooms, and green beans.
Combine all these ingredients and mix well.
Preheat the electric smoker to 250°F.
Make 4 cup-shaped containers from heavy duty aluminum foil.
Put vegetables in these cups.
Add herbs and spices to taste.
Pinch the top of foil cups together.
Make several holes in the foil so that the smoke can circulate around the vegetables.
Smoke for 1 hr. at 220°F.
Nutritional Information:
Calories: 97
Protein: 5.6g
Carbs: 14g
Fat: 9g

2. Herby Smoked Cauliflower

Prep time: 20 minutes
Servings: 4
Ingredients:
1 head cauliflower
Olive oil
Salt
Pepper
2 tsps. dried oregano
2 tsps. Dried basil
Preparations:
Start by soaking your woodchips for about an hour and preheating your smoker to 200°F/93°C.
Remove the woodchips from the liquid then pat dry before using.
Then take your cauliflower and chop into medium-sized pieces, removing the core. Place the pieces of cauliflower onto a sheet pan and then drizzle with the olive oil. Sprinkle the seasonings and herbs over the cauliflower then pop into the smoker. Smoke for 2 hours, checking and turning often.
Serve and enjoy!
Nutritional Information:
Calories: 31
Protein: 1.5g
Carbs: 6.7g
Fat: 0.34g

3. Smoked Green Beans with Lemon

Prep Time: 20 minutes
Serving 4
Ingredients
2 lbs. fresh green beans, trimmed and soaked
2 tbsps. Apple vinaigrette dressing
1 lemon
Preparations:
Place beans in a colander.
Preheat smoker to 140°F and add wood chips (recommended Oak wood chips).
Place the beans in the pan in a single layer and lightly coat with the dressing.
Place the beans on the upper shelf of the smoker and smoke for 1 hour.
Remove from the heat, cover with foil and let rest for 15 minutes.
Pour lemon juice, sprinkle with the lemon zest and serve.
Nutritional information:
Calories: 74.31
Total Fat: 0.66g
Total Carbs: 17.02g
Protein: 4.19g

4. Smoked Lemony-Garlic Artichokes

Prep time: 20 minutes
Servings: 4
Ingredients:
4 artichokes
4 minced garlic cloves
3 tbsps. Lemon juice
½ c. virgin olive oil
2 parsley sprigs
Sea salt
Preparations:
Put a large pot on your stove with a metal steaming basket inside.
Fill with water just to the bottom of the basket and bring to a boil.
Cut the artichoke tail and take out the toughest leaves.
With cooking shears, clip the pointy ends off of the outermost leaves.
Cut the artichokes in half lengthwise. Remove the hairy choke in the center.
Put the halves, stem side down, in the steamer basket. Reduce the heat to a rolling simmer.
On the pot, cover and steam for about 20 to 25 minutes, until the inside of the artichoke is tender.
Prepare a dressing: place in a mortar the garlic, lemon juice, olive oil, parsley, and salt.
Take away the basket and let the artichokes come to room temperature.
Preheat your smoker to 200°F.
Place the artichokes in aluminum foil packets and brush garlic mixture all over the artichokes.
Smoke the artichoke halves for approximately 1 hour.
Serve hot.
Nutritional information:
Calories: 83.22
Total Fat: 0.29g
Total Carbs: 18.82g
Protein: 5.54g

5. Smoked Portobello Mushrooms with Herbs de Provence

Prep time: 10 minutes
Servings: 4
Ingredients
12 large Portobello mushrooms
1 tbsp. Herbs de Provence
¼ c. extra virgin olive oil
Sea salt
Black pepper
Preparation:
Preheat smoker to 200°F and add wood chips (recommended oak wood chips).
In a bowl, mix Herbs de Provence, olive oil, salt, and pepper to taste.
Clean the mushrooms with a dry cloth or paper towel.
Rub the mushrooms all over with herbs mixture.
Place the mushrooms, cap side down, directly on the top grill rack. Smoke for approximately 2 hours.
Remove carefully so the herbal liquid in the cap remains in place.
Serve whole and enjoy!
Nutritional information:
Calories: 146.08
Fat: 13.63g
Total Carbs: 5.22g
Protein: 3.03g

6. Smoky Corn on the Cob

Prep time: 10 minutes
Servings: 5
Ingredients:
10 ears sweet corn
½ c. butter
Salt
Black pepper
Preparations:
Preheat your smoker to 225°F and add wood chips (recommended oak or hickory).
Put the ears of corn on the top 2 racks of the smoker and smoke for 2 hours.
Rotate the corn every 30 minutes.
Serve hot with butter, salt, and pepper.
Nutritional information:
Calories: 408.72
Total Fat: 22.27g
Total Carbs: 53.5g
Protein: 9.55g

7. Smoked Potato Salad

Prep time: 30 mins
Servings: 4
Ingredients:
3 eggs, hard-boiled
2 tbsps. cider vinegar
1 lb. russet potatoes
1 tbsp. Dijon mustard
½ c. red onion
⅓ c. light mayonnaise
Salt
Black pepper
Preparations:
Preheat the electric smoker to 225°F.
Put prepared wood chips in the wood tray — use mesquite chips for the best result.
Put peeled potatoes in a saucepan and cover with water. Put on the lid and bring to a boil.
Cook for 20 mins. Pat potatoes dry, and put them on paper towels.
Directly smoke potatoes on the racks for 2 hrs. as you add extra wood chips in a cycle of 45 mins.
Remove potatoes, let them cool.
Chop them well for the preparation of the salad.
Combine boiled eggs, onion, mayonnaise, pickles, mustard, pepper, salt, and vinegar. Mix all these ingredients well.
Add potatoes to the prepared mixture. Put in the fridge for several hrs. covered.
Nutritional information:
Calories: 209
Total Fat: 9g
Total Carbs: 30g
Protein: 3g

8. Smoked Volcano Potatoes

Prep time: 15 minutes.
Servings: 2
Ingredients:
2 russet potatoes
¾ c. sour cream.
1 c. cheddar cheese
2 tbsps. green onion
8 bacon strips
4 tbsps. butter
2 tbsps. olive oil
Salt
Preparation
Preheat the electric smoker to 250°F.
Wash potatoes, pierce using the fork.
Take the oil and salt and rub on the potatoes. Wrap the potatoes in foil and put in the smoker.
Smoke potatoes for 3 hrs.
Cut off the top of each potato and remove the potato flesh, leaving the shell empty.
Fry and crumble the bacon. Combine potato flesh with bacon, butter, sour cream, and cheese in a bowl.
Put the prepared filling in the potatoes, add some cheese on the top.
Wrap the potato with 2 bacon slices — for securing use toothpicks.
Smoke for another 1 hr.
Add green onions with a little sour cream on top (sour cream will give a special flavor to the potato).
Nutritional information:
Calories: 256
Total Fat: 39.3g
Total Carbs: 31.7g
Protein: 32.1g

9. Groovy smoked asparagus

Prep time: 5 minutes
Serving: 4
Ingredients:
1 bunch asparagus
2 tbsps. Olive oil
1 tsp. chopped garlic
Kosher salt
½ tsp. black pepper
Preparations:
Prepare the water pan of your smoker accordingly
Pre-heat your smoker to 275 degrees Fahrenheit/135 degree Celsius
Fill a medium-sized bowl with water and add 3-4 handfuls of woods and allow them to soak
Add the asparagus to a grill basket in a single layer
Drizzle olive oil on top and sprinkle garlic, pepper, and salt
Toss them well
Put the basket in your smoker
Add a few chips into the loading bay and keep repeating until all of the chips after every 20 minutes
Smoke for 60-90 minutes
Serve and enjoy!
Nutritional information:
Calories: 68
Total Fat: 4.1g
Total Carbs: 7.1g
Protein: 2.8g

10. Smoked Squash Casserole

Prep time: 40 minutes
Servings 2

Ingredients:

2½ lbs. yellow squash
2 tbsps. parsley flakes
2 eggs, beaten
1 medium yellow onion
1 sleeve saltine crackers
1 package Velveeta cheese
½ c. Alouette Sundried Tomato Basil cheese spread
¼ c. Alouette Garlic and Herb cheese spread
¼ c. mayonnaise
¾ tsp. hot sauce
¼ tsp. Cajun seasoning
½ c. butter
¼ tsp. salt
¼ tsp. black pepper

Preparations:

Preheat the electric smoker to 250°F.
Combine squash and onion in a large saucepan and add water to cover. Boil on medium heat until tender.
Drain and to this hot mixture, add Velveeta cheese, Alouette cheese, mayonnaise, parsley flakes, hot sauce, Cajun seasoning, salt, and pepper to taste.
Stir all together well.
Cool a little, add eggs and stir until mixed.
Melt butter in a saucepan.
Add crushed crackers to the butter and stir well. Combine ½ cup of butter-cracker mix with the squash mixture. Stir thoroughly.
Pour into a disposable aluminum foil pan. Top the squash with remaining butter and crackers. Cover the pan tightly with aluminum foil.
Put on the lower rack of the smoker and cook for 1 hr. Put one small handful of prepared wood chips in the wood tray for the best result use hickory.
After an hour, remove the foil from the casserole and cook for another 15 mins.

Nutritional information:

Calories: 190
Total Fat: 8g
Total Carbs: 23g
Protein: 7g

11. Smoked Eggplant

Prep Time: 20 minutes.
Servings: 4
Ingredients:
2 medium eggplant
Olive oil
Preparations:
Preheat your smoker to 200°F/93°C and soak your wood chips for an hour.
Remove the woodchips from the liquid then pat dry before using.
Then carefully peel your eggplant then slice into rounds of around ¼"/1cm thick.
Brush each of these rounds with olive oil then place directly into the smoker.
Smoke for approximately an hour until soft and tender. Serve and enjoy!
Nutritional Information:
Calories: 85
Protein: 1.6g
Carbs: 9.4g
Fat: 4.6g

12. Twice Pulled Potatoes

Prep time 30 minutes.
Servings 4
Ingredients:
1 lb. pulled pork
2 russet potatoes
1/3 c. sour cream
4 oz. cream cheese
1/3 c. cheddar cheese
Chives
BBQ sauce, to taste
Preparations:
Preheat the electric smoker to 225°F. Smoke washed potatoes for 2 hours.
Mix potato flesh, cheddar cheese, sour cream, cream cheese, pulled pork and BBQ sauce in a bowl and stir well.
Put prepared mixture back into potatoes skins.
Smoke for another 40 mins.
Season with more BBQ sauce, if desired. Sprinkle some cheddar cheese and chives on the top.

Nutritional Information:
Calories: 285
Protein: 3g
Carbs: 24.1g
Fat: 8.1g

Chapter 8: Snacks & Desserts

1. Grilled Apple Pie

Prep Time: 10 minutes.
Servings: 6
Ingredients:
5 apples
¼ c. sugar
1 tbsp. cornstarch
Flour
1 refrigerated pie crust
¼ c. peach preserve
Preparations:
Let your smoker be set to 275 degrees F and soak your wood chips for an hour.
Remove the wood chips from the liquid then pat dry before using.
Then take a medium bowl and add the apples, sugar, and cornstarch then stir well until combined.
Pop to one side.
Dust the work surface using flour before rolling out the pie crust.
Place the pie crust into a pie pan without greasing it first.
Spread the preserve into the bottom of the pie, then top with apple slices.
Pop into the smoker and cook for 30-40 minutes until bubbly and brown. Remove from the smoker, let it rest for 10 minutes then serve and enjoy!
Nutritional information:
Calories: 236
Protein: 2.2g
Carbs: 39.8g
Fat: 8.4g

2. Pear and Fig Upside Down Cake

Prep Time: 20 minutes.
Serves: 8
Ingredients:
For the cake
1 tbsp. unsalted butter
¼ tsp. salt
9 tbsps. Unsalted butter
3 free-range eggs
1 tsp. vanilla
1½ c. Cake flour
¾ tsp. baking powder
¾ c. Granulated sugar
¼ tsp. baking soda
8 tbsps. sour cream
For the fruit and glaze
1 pear
4 grapes
4 tbsps. Unsalted butter
½ c. brown sugar

Preparations:
Preheat your smoker to 250°F and soak your wood chips for an hour.
Remove the wood chips from the liquid then pat dry before using.
Next grab a 10" (25cm) cake pan and grease well with butter.
Take a medium bowl and cream the butter and sugar together.
Place the fruit into the bottom of the cake pan, then put the sugar and butter mixture (from the fruit and glaze ingredients) over the top.
Pop to one side. Next take another bowl and add sugar and butter, then beat until fluffy and light.
Add vanilla and eggs then beat for another minute.
Lastly, add the salt, baking powder, sour cream and flour then stir well to combine.
Pour this cake batter over the fruit then pop into the smoker.
Cook for 35-45 minutes until cooked through. Remove from the smoker, rest for 10 minutes then serve and enjoy.

Nutritional information:
Calories: 385
Protein: 6.8g
Carbs: 48.2g
Fat: 18.6g

3. Belgian Beer Brownies

Prep Time: 20 minutes.

Servings: 15

Ingredients:

1 c. stout beer
2 c. all-purpose white flour
10 oz. chocolate
4 c. granulated sugar
1/8 tsp. salt

Confectioner's sugar
4 oz. bittersweet eating chocolate
2 c. butter
8 large eggs
2 tsp. pure vanilla extract

Preparations:
If Three Philosophers ale is what you are using, then pour into a heavy-bottomed saucepan.
Place the saucepan over high heat. Bring to the boil. Keep boiling till it reduces to half its original quantity.
Transfer into a heatproof dish. If stout is what you are using, then need not boil it and pour into a heatproof dish.
Toss bittersweet chocolate and 2 tbsps. flour in a bowl and set aside.
Wipe the saucepan clean and place it back on low heat. Add butter.
When the butter melts, use a little of it and grease a large baking dish.
Place the dish in the refrigerator for 5-6 minutes.
Remove the dish from the refrigerator and sprinkle 1-2 tbsps flour all over the buttered area.
Add unsweetened chocolate to the saucepan and melt the chocolate stirring constantly. Remove from heat.
Whisk together eggs and granulated sugar in a bowl
Add the ale or stout and whisk again
Add vanilla, salt and melted chocolate and whisk again.
Add remaining flour and fold gently. Add chocolate chunks and fold again.
Pour the batter into the prepared baking dish. Alternately, you can pour into a cast iron skillet.
Preheat the smoker to 275°F following the manufacturer's instructions.
Place the baking dish in the smoker and smoke for about 40 minutes or a toothpick when inserted in the center comes out clean.
Remove from the smoker and cool completely. Cut into 24 squares and serve.

Nutritional information:

Calories: 486
Protein: 4.1g

Carbs: 54.7g
Fat: 27.4g

4. Baked Lemon Meringue Pie

Prep time: 20 minutes.
Servings: 8
Ingredients:
For filling:
1½ c. sugar
2/3 c. lemon juice
1 tbsp. lemon zest
Salt
4 tbsps. unsalted butter
3 free range eggs + 3 egg yolks
For Pie:
1 pie dough
1 tbsp. heavy cream
1 free range egg
For meringue:
3 egg whites
5 tbsps. sugar
1 tsp. vanilla extract
Preparations:
Preheat your smoker to 250°F/120°C and soak your wood chips for an hour.
Remove the wood chips from the liquid then pat dry before using.
Take a medium bowl and add the sugar, lemon juice, lemon zest and salt.
Stir well to combine. Next pour this mixture onto a greased baking sheet then place into your smoker for 30 minutes.
Remove from the smoker and set to one side.
Turn up the temperature of your smoker 275°F and grease your pie dish.
Sprinkle your work surface with flour and start to roll out the pie dough until it's approximately 1/8" (1/4 cm).
Place into the pie dish then push down well.
Pop into the freezer for 30 minutes.
Take a bowl and add the cream and one of the eggs. Stir well to combine then brush over the edges of the pie.
Transfer the pie to the smoker and cook for 10 minutes.
Remove and allow it to cool.

Now let's make the filling.

Take a large bowl and add 3 eggs and 3 egg yolks (keep hold of whites), whisk, and stir in the lemon mixture.

Mix well. Using a Bain Marie or double boiler, warm the lemon mixture for 10 minutes until it thickens nicely. Keep stirring.

Remove this filling from the heat and whisk in the butter.

Dispense the lemon mixture into the pie crust and place back into the smoker for 20 minutes until the filling has set.

Cool overnight in the fridge. Finally, make the meringue! Place the egg whites into a bowl with the sugar then place in a Bain Marie or double boiler to warm through. Keep stirring until the sugar has dissolved.

Remove from the heat then beat with a whisk until the egg whites are white and fluffy. Add the vanilla then beat again. Pipe the meringue mixture onto the top of the pie then use a kitchen torch to brown the top. Serve and enjoy!

Nutritional information:

Calories: 307

Protein: 4.7g

Carbs: 39.8g

Fat: 14.6g

5. Smoked Peaches

Prep time: 10 minutes.
Servings: 6
Ingredients:
6 fresh peaches.
1 c. wood chips of your choice
Preparations:
Preheat your smoker to 200°F/93°C and soak the wood chips for an hour.
Remove the wood chips from the liquid then pat dry before using.
Place the peaches directly into your smoker and cook for 30 minutes – the first 20 with the skin down, the final 10 with the skin up.
Remove from the smoker, and serve warm with meats, in salads or even as a special way to round off your meal.
Nutritional information:
Calories: 117
Protein: 2.7g
Carbs: 28.6g
Fat: 0.8g

6. Smoked Apple Crumble

Prep time: 10 minutes.
Servings: 15
Ingredients:
For the pie filling:
3 tsps. All-purpose flour
1 tsp. ground cinnamon
1 c. sugar
3 lbs. apples
For crumble:
2 c. rolled oats
½ tsp. baking powder
½ tsp. baking soda
1 c. butter
2 c. brown sugar
Ice cream to serve
Preparation:
Preheat the smoker to 275°F following the manufacturer's instructions.
Make the pie filling as follows: Mix together in a bowl all the pie-filling ingredients and toss well.
Transfer into 14-15 ramekins (2/3 fill it). Do not grease the ramekins.
To make crumble: Mix together in a bowl flour, brown sugar, oats, baking powder and baking soda. Pour butter over it and mix well.
Place about ¼ cup of this mixture over each of the ramekins (over the apple filling).
Place the ramekins on the center rack in the smoker and smoke for an hour.
Remove the ramekins from the smoker and invert onto individual serving bowls. Serve as it is or with a scoop of ice cream.
Nutritional information:
Calories: 267
Protein: 2.6g
Carbs: 41.4g
Fat: 13.3g

7. Smoke Roasted Apple Crisp

Prep Time: 15 minutes.
Servings: 12

Ingredients:
12 sweet apples
3 tbsps. Lemon juice
3 tbsps. Arrowroot
12 tbsps. Butter
¾ tsp. lemon zest, grated
1½ c. sugar
1/8 tsp. salt
3 tsp. ground cinnamon
¾ c. granola
¾ c. flour
¾ c. brown sugar.
Apple ice cream of cinnamon ice cream to serve

Preparations:
Place apples in a glass bowl
Add lemon juice and lemon zest and toss well.
Add 2/3-c. sugar, 2 tsp. ground cinnamon and arrowroot and toss well.
Taste and adjust the sugar if required.
Transfer into a cast iron skillet and set aside.
Add rest of the ingredients except ice cream into the food processor bowl and pulse until the mixture is coarse in texture. Do not pulse for long.
Sprinkle this mixture over the apples in the skillet.
Preheat the smoker to 275°F following the manufacturer's instructions.
Place the cast iron skillet in the smoker.
Smoke until the mixture is crisp and golden brown on top. It should take 45-60 minutes.
Remove from the smoker and cool for a while.
Serve warm as it is or with ice cream.

Nutritional Information:
Calories: 341   Fat: 11.9g
Protein: 1.5g
Carbs: 61.1g

8. Tangerine Smoked Flans

Prep Time: 15 minutes.
Servings: 10
Ingredients:
For caramel:
½ c. water
2 c. sugar
For flan:
1 c. sugar
4 large egg yolks
6 large eggs
1/8 tsp. salt
2 c. half and half
2 tsps. Vanilla extract
2 cinnamon sticks
2 ½ c. whole milk
12 strips tangerine zest
Preparation:
To make caramel:
Place a heavy saucepan over high heat.
Add sugar and water and stir.
Cover and cook for 2 minutes. Lower heat to medium and uncover.
Cook until the sugar caramelizes and is golden brown in color. Do not stir during this process.
Remove from heat and pour into 10-12 ramekins. Wear kitchen gloves and swirl the ramekins so that the caramelized sugar coats the bottom as well as the sides.
Set aside the ramekins to cool. It will harden.
Set your ramekins on a baking sheet that is rimmed.
Meanwhile make the flan as follows:
Add eggs, yolks, sugar and salt in a large heatproof bowl and whisk until well combined. Place a heavy saucepan over medium heat.
Add milk, half and half, tangerine zest, cinnamon and vanilla bean.
Heat for a few minutes until warm.
Remove from heat.
Add about ½ cup of this mixture into the bowl of eggs and whisk.

Continue this process until all the milk mixture is added to the egg mixture, whisking each time.

Add vanilla essence if using and whisk again. Cool for a while and pour into the ramekins

Preheat the smoker to 250°F following the manufacturer's instructions.

Place the baking sheet with ramekin cups in the smoker. Smoke for around 1 ½ hours or until the flan is set.

Remove from the smoker and cool completely. Chill for 5-6 hours in the refrigerator.

To serve: Run a knife around the edges of the flan. Invert onto a plate and serve.

Nutritional Information:

Calories: 315

Protein: 6.3g

Carbs: 49g

Fat: 10.5g

9. Pizza Jalapeño Poppers

Prep Time: 20 minutes.
Servings: 6
Ingredients:
12 Jalapeño peppers
8 oz. Cream cheese
4 oz. Cheddar cheese
4 oz. Mozzarella cheese
2 Bread heel slices
12 Bacon slices
Preparations:
Preheat your smoker to 200°F/93°C and soak your wood chips for an hour.
Remove the woodchips from the liquid then pat dry before using.
Pop the cheeses into the food processor and hit the button. Blend until smooth.
Next cut the stems off the peppers, scoop out the seeds and fill the inside of the pepper with the cheese mixture.
Tear out a small piece of bread from the crusts and pop them into the end of the pepper to prevent the cheese to ooze out when it warms.
Now wrap the bacon around the pepper and hold in place with toothpicks.
Place directly into your smoker and cook for an hour.
Check after the half an hour and turn. Leave longer if required.
Nutritional Information:
Calories: 63
Protein: 2g
Carbs: 6.3g
Fat: 3.7g

10. Smoked Chocolate Bread Pudding

Prep time: 20 minutes.
Servings: 15

Ingredients:

2 lbs. brioche
4 c. whole milk
1/8 tsp. salt
16 oz. bittersweet chocolate
4 large egg yolks
8 large eggs
2 tsp. vanilla extract
2 vanilla beans
6 c. heavy whipping cream
Butter
3 c. sugar
Smoked ice cream

Preparation:

Preheat the smoker to 250°F following the manufacturer's instructions.

Take a large disposable aluminum foil and place the bread cubes in it in a single layer. Place the pan in the smoker and smoke for 30-45 minutes until the bread cubes are toasted.

Meanwhile, add eggs, yolks, vanilla extract and salt in a large heatproof bowl and whisk until well combined.

Place a heavy saucepan over medium heat. Add milk, cream, sugar and vanilla bean as well as its seeds.

Heat for a few minutes until hot and the sugar is dissolved Remove from heat.

Add half the chocolate and stir constantly until it melts. Cool for a while.

Add about ½ cup of this mixture into the bowl of eggs and whisk constantly. Continue this process until all the milk mixture is added to the egg mixture, whisking each time.

Add vanilla essence if using and whisk again.

Add the toasted bread cubes into it and stir.

Grease a cast iron skillet with butter. Pour the entire mixture into the skillet.

Sprinkle remaining chocolate pieces on it. Preheat the smoker to 275°F following the manufacturer's instructions.

Place the skillet in the smoker. Smoke for around 45 minutes to 1-½ hours (depending on what temperature you have set the smoker) or until set.

Remove from the smoker and serve hot with smoked ice cream.

Nutritional Information:

Calories: 780
Protein: 14.6g
Carbs: 67.6g
Fat: 50.5g

11. Smoked Banana Foster

Prep time: 10 minutes
Servings: 10
Ingredients:
10 overripe bananas, peeled, halved lengthwise
Rum and raisin sauce to serve
Preparation:
Preheat the smoker to 250°F following the manufacturer's instructions.
Take a large disposable aluminum foil and place the bananas on it in a single layer.
Smoke for 15-20 minutes.
Serve with rum and raisin sauce.
Nutritional Information:
Calories: 355
Protein: 1g
Carbs: 41g
Fat: 12g

12. Smoke Roasted Berry Crisp

Prep time: 15 minutes
Servings: 6

Ingredients:
6 pints blueberries
1 c. granulated sugar
4 tbsps. Lemon juice
1 c. brown sugar
¾ c. cold unsalted butter
1½ c. all-purpose flour
1/8 tsp. Salt
2 tsps. Lemon zest
1 c. gingersnap cookies
Vanilla ice cream to serve

Preparation:
Place blueberries in a glass bowl.
Add lemon juice and lemon zest and toss well.
Add ½ cup flour and toss well. Taste and adjust the sugar if required.
Transfer into a cast iron skillet and set aside.
Add rest of the ingredients except ice cream into the food processor bowl and pulse until the mixture is coarse in texture. Do not pulse for long.
Dust this mixture over the blueberries in the skillet.
Preheat the smoker to 275°F following the manufacturer's instructions.
Place the cast iron skillet in the smoker.
Smoke until the mixture is crisp and golden brown on top. It should take 45-60 minutes.
Remove from the smoker and cool for a while.
Serve either warm or with ice cream.

Nutritional Information:
Calories: 660
Protein: 7g
Carbs: 103g
Fat: 25g

Chapter 9: Delicious Cheese & Nuts

1. Smoked Cheddar Cheese

Prep time: 5 mins
Servings: 8
Ingredients:
2 x 8 oz. blocks Cheddar cheese
Preparation:
Preheat your smoker to a low temperature – make sure it's no higher than 90°F (32°C) to make sure cheese doesn't melt all over the place. Soak the wood chips for an hour. Remove the wood chips from the liquid then pat dry before using.
Now place your blocks of cheese directly on the grate and smoke for around 4 hours. Remove the cheese from the smoker, cool to room temp and place into a container, before popping it into the fridge for two weeks. This allows the flavor to really develop.
Serve and enjoy.
Nutritional Information:
Calories: 220.1
Protein: 14g
Carbs: 0g
Fat: 18g

2. Smoked Brie Cheese

Prep time: 5 mins
Servings: 8
Ingredients:
8 oz. blocks Brie cheese
Preparation:
Preheat your smoker to a low temperature – make sure it's no higher than 90°F (32°C). Soak the wood chips for an hour. Remove the wood chips from the liquid then pat dry before using.
Now add your cheese blocks to the smoker grate and allow to smoke for about 4 hours. Remove from heat and set to cool to room temp.
Place into a container, before popping it into the fridge for two weeks. This allows the flavor to really develop. Serve and enjoy.
Nutritional Information:
Calories: 100
Protein: 4g
Carbs: 0g
Fat: 9g

3. Grilled Smoked Bananas with Dark Chocolate and Toasted Hazelnuts

Prep time: 10 mins
Servings: 4
Ingredients:
4 small semi-ripe bananas
½ tsp. sea salt
3 tbsps. chopped dark chocolate
6 tsps. chopped hazelnuts
Vanilla ice cream
Preparation:
Preheat your smoker to 250°F/120°C and soak your wood chips for an hour.
Remove the wood chips from the liquid then pat dry before using.
Peel the banana in half so that the top part of the banana is exposed but the bottom is still sitting in its skin.
Make a few slits in the banana then place into your smoker for 5 minutes.
Remove the bananas from the smoker then sprinkle with salt, chocolate and topped nuts. Serve with a generous scoop of ice-cream and enjoy.
Nutritional Information:
Calories: 241
Protein: 3.8g
Carbs: 39.8g
Fat: 9.3g

4. Garlic and Cayenne Almonds

Prep time: 5 mins
Servings: 3
Ingredients:
1 lb. raw almonds
2 tbsps. melted butter
1 tbsp. salt
1 tsp. garlic powder
½ tsp. cayenne pepper
Preparation:
Preheat your smoker to 250°F/120°C and soak the wood chips for an hour.
Remove the wood chips from the liquid then pat dry before using.
Now grab a medium bowl and add the melted butter, salt, garlic and cayenne, then stir well to combine.
Add the almonds, and stir well to coat, then transfer to a sheet pan, spreading thinly. Smoke for 2 hours until crispy and dry.
Remove the nuts from the smoker, cool completely in the pan, then serve and enjoy.
Nutritional Information:
Calories: 160
Protein: 5g
Carbs: 9g
Fat: 13g

5. Splendid Cheeseburger Patty

Prep time: 10 mins
Servings: 8
Ingredients:
1½ lbs. beef, ground
1 lb. bacon slices
1 tsp. garlic powder
1 tsp. salt
1 tsp. pepper
1 tsp. onion powder
4 tbsps. A1 sauce
½ c. shredded cheddar cheese
½ c. mozzarella cheese
¾ c. grated carrots
12 hamburger dill sliced pickles
Preparation:
Add salt, onion powder, garlic powder and 2 tablespoons of A1 sauce with the ground beef and blend thoroughly. Put the beef in a Ziploc bag and spread it evenly so that the beef resembles a blanket. Put the beef in the fridge to chill for some time.
Make a bacon weave with the bacon strips and set aside.
Cut the Ziploc bag and remove the plastic cover from the be3ef blanket. Layer the remaining A1 sauce, cheese, carrot and pickle over the blanket and fold it tightly to make a roll. Make sure that there are no holes.
Now, place the beef roll at the centre of the bacon weave and fold the weave tightly, making sure that there are no holes.
Put the fatty inside the smoker and cook for 2 hours at 225 degrees.
Slice into desired sizes and serve with sauce.
Nutritional Information:
Calories: 320
Carbs: 1g
Fat: 26g
Protein: 21g

6. Marvelous Smoked Mac'n'Cheese

Prep time: 15 mins
Servings: 6
Ingredients:
16 oz. elbow macaroni
¼ c. butter
¼ c. all-purpose flour
3 c. milk
8 oz. cream cheese
1 tsp. salt
½ tsp. black pepper
16 oz. shredded sharp cheddar cheese
16 oz. shredded gouda cheese
8 oz. shredded parmesan cheese
Preparation:
Preheat the smoker to 225 degrees and fill the wood tray with wood chips.
Cook the pasta according to the directions mentioned in the package. Melt butter in a saucepan and whisk flour into the butter. Cook for 2 minutes over medium heat and make sure that the butter sauce becomes thick and bubbly. Whisk in milk and bring it to a boil. Cook until turns thick and then add cream cheese and make the mixture smooth. Remember to season with salt and pepper.
Take a large bowl to combine 1 cup cheddar cheese, 1 cup gouda cheese and the parmesan cheese along with the pasta, cream sauce and bacon cubes. Pour this mixture in aluminium roasting pan and sprinkle the remaining portions of cheddar cheese and gouda cheese on top.
Place the pan in the smoker and smoke for one hour at 225 degrees. Make sure that the cheese top becomes brown and bubbly.
Serve warm.
Nutrition Information:
Calories: 677
Carbs: 52.7g
Protein: 31.6g
Fat: 38.3g

7. Macaroni & Cheese

Prep time: 30 mins
Servings: 8
Ingredients:
16 oz. medium pasta shells
¼ c. butter
¼ c. flour
3 c. milk
½ tsp. onion powder
Salt
Black pepper
8 oz. grated Colby cheese
2 oz. grated cheddar cheese
1 c. breadcrumbs

Preparation:
Cook pasta according to package directions until al dente and drain.
While the pasta is cooking, prepare the sauce. Melt butter in a large saucepan over medium heat. Whisk flour into butter until smooth and add milk in a thin stream, whisking constantly. Stir in onion powder, salt and pepper and heat sauce mixture to a boil, stirring occasionally. Reduce heat and simmer until sauce is thickened, stirring constantly, about 2 minutes. Remove sauce from heat, add Colby cheese and stir until cheese is melted.
Spray a 3-quart casserole with nonstick cooking spray. Add pasta to sauce, stir until coated and pour into casserole dish. In a small bowl, toss cheddar cheese with bread crumbs and sprinkle over macaroni & cheese.
Place casserole dish on top grate of Masterbuilt smoker preheated to 225°F and smoke until browned and bubbly, about 1 hour. Serve immediately and enjoy!

Nutritional Information:
Calories: 467
Fat: 21g
Protein: 20g
Carbs: 49g

8. Smoked Chorizo Queso

Prep time: 10 mins
Servings: 10
Ingredients:
16 oz. cubed Velveeta cheese
4 oz. Cream cheese, cubed
10 oz. Rotel
1 lb. cooked Chorizo, chopped
Preparation:
Set your smoker to preheat to 250°F with apple wood chips.
Combine all your ingredients in an aluminum pan then set to smoke until your cheese completely melts (about 1 hour, stirring every 15 minutes).
Serve with tortilla chips. Enjoy!
Nutritional Information:
Calories: 372
Protein: 19.2g
Carbs: 5.4g
Fat: 30.3g

9. Christy's Smoked Pimento Cheese Appetizer

Prep time: 10 mins
Servings: 6
Ingredients:
1 lb. Kielbasa sausage
Sliced jalapeño peppers
Saltine crackers
12 oz. Pimento Cheese Dip
Preparation:
Set smoker to preheat to 225°F. Set your sausages to smoke for 45 mins - 1 hour then set aside.
Arrange your cheese and crackers on a serving platter, slice your sausages and set on top of the cheese while still hot.
Lace saltine crackers on a platter, salt-side down. Garnish with Jalapeños and serve!
Nutritional Information:
Calories: 364
Protein: 23.5g
Carbs: 13.5g
Fat: 25.8g

10. Smoked Rosemary Cashews

Prep time: 5 mins
Servings: 3
Ingredients:
2 c. cashews
1 tsp. packed light brown sugar
1 tsp. rosemary
¼ tsp. mustard powder
2 tsps. olive oil
Preparation:
Preheat your smoker to 250°F/120°C and soak the woodchips for an hour.
Remove the woodchips from the liquid then pat dry before using.
Next, take a medium bowl and add the sugar, rosemary and mustard powder. Stir well to combine, then add the oil.
Next throw in the nuts and stir well to combine.
Spread in a single layer onto a sheet pan and place into your smoker.
Cook for 30 minutes until crispy and dry, or longer if they're not quite done yet.
Remove from the smoker, cool in the pan, then serve and enjoy.
Nutritional information:
Calories: 160
Protein: 4g
Carbs: 9g
Fat: 13g

11. Smoked Pecans

Prep time: 20 mins
Servings: 4
Ingredients:
2 c. pecans, shelled
1 tbsp. olive oil
1 serving Pecan Spice Blend
Preparation:
Start by setting up your smoker and preheating to 250°F/120°C. Soak the wood chips for an hour.
Remove the woodchips from the liquid then pat dry before using.
Grab a medium bowl and add to it the olive oil, plus the pecan spice blend, followed by the nuts. Stir well to combine and completely coat the nuts.
Pour the nuts onto a sheet pan and pop into the smoker.
Smoke for around 30-60 minutes, until the nuts are crispy and brown. You might want to stir or shake them often to help them smoke evenly.
Remove from the smoker and cool to room temperature before serving.
Enjoy!
Nutritional Information:
Calories: 2.7
Protein: 15.2g
Carbs: 3.8g
Fat: 20.8g

12. Smoked Spiced Nuts and Seeds

Prep time: 10 mins
Servings: 4
Ingredients:
½ c. raw almonds
½ c. cashews
½ c. walnuts
½ c. pumpkin seeds
2 tsps. grapeseed oil
1 tsp. pure maple syrup
½ tsp. sea salt
½ tsp. thyme, dried
½ tsp. rosemary, dried
¼ tsp. cayenne pepper, ground

Preparation:
Before you do anything else, pop the nuts into filtered water to soak and leave overnight.
Preheat your smoker to 225F/110C and soak the woodchips for one hour.
Remove the woodchips from the liquid then pat dry before using.
Drain the nuts and pat them dry using a clean tea towel or paper towels. Pop to one side for a moment.
Grab a large bowl and combine the oil, maple syrup and spices, then stir well to combine.
Throw in the nuts and stir through to make sure they're well-coated.
Spread the nuts onto a sheet pan and pop inside your smoker.
Leave them for the 60 minutes, then test for crunchiness. If they're not dry and crunchy, leave them in longer.
Then serve and enjoy. But a word of warning; they won't last long!

Nutritional Information:
Calories: 2.7
Protein: 15.2g
Carbs: 3.8g
Fat: 20.8g

Chapter 10: Sauces & Rubs as Bonus (Not Made By Smoker)

1. Texas Style Brisket Rub

Prep time: 5 minutes
Servings: 3
Ingredients:
6 tbsps. salt
2 tbsps. black pepper
4 tbsps. garlic powder
10 tbsps. paprika
6 tbsps. onion powder
2 tsps. mild chili powder
1 tsp. ground coriander
4 tsps. ground cumin
2 tsps. dried oregano
1 tsp. garlic powder
½ tsp. cayenne pepper
Preparations:
Combine the ingredients in a bowl and store in an airtight container.
Store in a cool dark place. It can last for 6 months.
Use as much as required.
Nutritional Information:
Calories: 18
Protein: 0g
Carbs: 5g
Fat: 0.5g

2. Montreal Steak Rub

Prep time: 5 minutes.
Servings: 3
Ingredients:
2 tbsps. salt
2 tbsps. Black pepper
2 tbsp. paprika
1 tbsp. red pepper flakes
1 tbsp. coriander
1 tbsp. dill
1 tbsp. garlic powder
1 tbsp. onion powder
Preparation:
Simply place all ingredients into an airtight jar,
Stir well to combine then close.
Use within six months.
Nutrition information
Calories: 10
Protein: 1.2g
Carbs: 3.2g
Fat: 0.1g

3. Sage BBQ Rub

Prep time: 5 minutes.
Servings: 3
Ingredients:
¾ c. paprika
½ c. sugar
½ c. salt
¼ c. black pepper
2 tbsps. thyme
2 tbsps. dry mustard
1 tbsp. cumin
1 tbsp. cayenne pepper
1 tbsp. sage
Preparation:
Simply place all ingredients into an airtight jar,
Stir well to combine then close.
Use within six months.
Nutrition information
Calories: 40
Protein: 3.2g
Carbs: 2.2g
Fat: 1g

4. Carolina Barbeque Rub

Prep Time: 5 minutes.
Servings: 2
Ingredients:
2 tbsps. Salt.
2 tbsps. Black pepper
2 tbsps. White sugar
¼ c. Paprika
2 tbsps. Brown sugar
2 tbsps. Cumin
2 tbsps. Chili powder
Preparations:
Simply place all ingredients into an airtight jar,
Stir well to combine then close.
Use within six months.
Nutrition information.
Calories: 30
Protein: 1.6g
Carbs: 3.2g
Fat: 0.2g

5. Memphis Rub

Prep Time: 5 mins.
Servings: 4
Ingredients:
½ c. paprika
¼ c. garlic powder
¼ c. mild chili powder
3 tbsps. salt
3 tbsps. black pepper
2 tbsps. onion powder
2 tbsps. celery seeds
1 tbsps. brown sugar
1 tbsp. dried oregano
1 tbsp. dried thyme
1 tbsp. cumin
2 tsps. dry mustard
2 tsps. ground coriander
2 tsps. ground allspice
Preparations:
Simply place all ingredients into an airtight jar,
Stir well to combine then close.
Use within six months.
Nutritional information:
Calories: 40
Protein: 1.7g
Carbs: 4.2g
Fat: 1.1g

6. Black Bean & Sesame Sauce

Prep time: 5 minutes
Servings: 4
Ingredients:
½ can black beans
1 tsp. soft dark brown sugar
2 tsp. honey
1 tsp. Chinese five-spice powder
½ tsp. grated ginger
1 red chili
2 tsps. tahini
2 tbsps. cider vinegar
2 tsps. soy sauce
5 tbsps. water
Salt
Pepper

Preparations:
Start by opening up your food processor and throwing in all the ingredients.
Heat the button, blend until smooth then pour the sauce into a saucepan.
Cook over medium heat for 5 minutes until glossy and thick, stirring continuously.
Nutritional Information:
Calories: 10
Protein: 1.2g
Carbs: 3.2g
Fat: 0.1g

7. Best-Ever Chili Sauce

Prep time: 5 minutes.
Servings: 4
Ingredients:
2 tbsps. vinegar
1 tbsp. ginger
1 tbsp. olive oil
½ tsp. chipotle powder
6 marinated cherry peppers
4 whole San Marzano tomatoes
1 garlic clove
1 large scallion
½ red pepper
Salt
Pepper
Preparation:
This one is very easy!
Mix all the ingredients into a food processor and blend until smooth.
Serve and enjoy!
Nutritional Information:
Calories: 10
Protein: 1.2g
Carbs: 3.2g
Fat: 0.1g

8. Quick Red Wine Sauce

Prep time: 5 minutes.
Ingredients:
1 c. Beef stock
½ c. Red wine
2 c. Brown sugar
1 tsp. Balsamic vinegar
Salt
Pepper
Preparation:
Start by placing the beef stock into a saucepan and place over medium heat. Simmer until reduced to half.
Next add the remaining ingredients, then stir to combine.
Continue cooking for another 10 minutes or so until the sauce has reduced to half again.
 Remove from the heat, season to taste then serve and enjoy!
Nutritional Information:
Calories: 10
Protein: 1.2g
Carbs: 3.2g
Fat: 0.1g

9. Easy Mustard Sauce

Prep time: 5 minutes.
Servings: 3
Ingredients:
1 tbsp. Butter
1 chopped Onion
1 minced garlic clove
1 c. Dijon mustard
¾ c. Brown sugar
¾ c. White distilled vinegar
1 tbsp. hot sauce
Salt
Pepper
Preparation:
Start by placing the butter into a saucepan and placing over medium heat.
When the butter has melted, add the garlic and onions and allow to cook until soft.
 Add the remaining ingredients, stir well to combine then reduce the heat.
Allow it to simmer (uncovered) for around 10 minutes until the sauce starts to thicken.
Season to taste, add any extra chili sauce you might like and stir through.
Cool to room temperature before serving. Then enjoy!
Nutritional Information:
Calories: 10
Protein: 1.2g
Carbs: 3.2g
Fat: 0.1g

10. Teriyaki Sauce

Prep Time: 5 mins.
Servings: 3
Ingredients:
5 tbsps. soy sauce
3 tbsps. sake
2 tbsps. mirin
½ tsp. ginger
1 tsp. honey
1 sliced spring onion
Salt
Pepper
Preparation:
Place the honey, ginger, mirin, sake and soy sauce into a bowl and stir well to combine.
Transfer this into a small saucepan and place over medium heat.
Simmer until thickened, then remove from the heat.
Add the spring onion and stir well until combined.
Season with salt and pepper to taste, then serve and enjoy.
Nutritional Information:
Calories: 107
Protein: 6g
Carbs: 16g
Fat: 0.1g

Conclusion

We have tried to collect some of the most fascinating and easy to cook smoked food recipes for you. We hope that you will have great experience cooking with your new Masterbuilt smoker when you follow these recipes.

We look forward to bringing you more delicious and extraordinary cooking guides in days to come.

Made in the USA
Middletown, DE
05 September 2018